Collins Big Cat

Assessment and Support Guide F

Series editor: Cliff Moon

William Collins' dream of knowledge for all began with the publication of his first book in 1819. A self-educated mill worker, he not only enriched millions of lives, but also founded a flourishing publishing house. Today, staying true to this spirit, Collins books are packed with inspiration, innovation and practical expertise. They place you at the centre of a world of possibility and give you exactly what you need to explore it.

Published by Collins
An imprint of HarperCollins*Publishers*
77–85 Fulham Palace Road
Hammersmith
London
W6 8JB

Browse the complete Collins catalogue at
www.collinseducation.com

© HarperCollins*Publishers* Limited 2009

10 9 8 7 6 5

ISBN-13 978-0-00-723112-6

British Library Cataloguing in Publication Data
A Catalogue record for this publication is available from the British Library

Credits
Authors: Clare Dowdall and Linda Pagett
Scottish curriculum advisor: Eleanor McMillan
Series editor: Cliff Moon
Design managers: Nicola Whitehorn and Nicola Kenwood
Designer: Neil Adams
Illustrations: Steph Dix
Photographs: Sarah Loader

Printed and bound by Martins the Printers Ltd

Get the latest Collins Big Cat news at
www.collinsbigcat.com

Mixed Sources
Product group from well-managed
forests and other controlled sources
www.fsc.org Cert no. SW-COC-1806
© 1996 Forest Stewardship Council

FSC is a non-profit international organisation established to promote the responsible management of the world's forests. Products carrying the FSC label are independently certified to assure consumers that they come from forests that are managed to meet the social, economic and ecological needs of present and future generations.

Find out more about HarperCollins and the environment at
www.harpercollins.co.uk/green

Contents

A Letter from Cliff Moon

Series editor, *Collins Big Cat*

Dear Colleague

I'd like to start with a parable, paraphrased from Robert O'Brien's 1971 children's novel, *Mrs Frisby and the Rats of NIMH* (Puffin Modern Classics):

> Once upon a time a group of laboratory rats learnt to read. First they were taught letters and their associated sounds but that didn't mean a great deal because, as the rats said, "we didn't know what reading was" and "as to what all this was for, none of us had any inkling".
>
> But then one day the penny dropped. The rats saw a sign which said "R-A-T-S", remembered the picture which went with the word, and realised what reading was: ... "using symbols to suggest a picture or an idea". Eventually they were able to read the instructions for opening their cages and that led to their escape ...
>
> **"By teaching us to read, [the scientists] had taught us how to get away."**

Now there's a purpose for teaching reading. Everything we do about reading should help children to *get away*; away into a world of fantasy, away into information gathering, and away into seeing the world through others' eyes. If we only have a single aim in teaching reading then it should be to get children to want to read under the bedclothes with a torch (figuratively speaking). That implies their having access to reading material which is worth the effort and books they can't put down.

How do we learn?

There is little evidence to suggest that we learn different things in different ways. Take riding a bike, for instance. When you learn to ride a bike you don't do discrete exercises in ankle movements, leg pushing, handlebar gripping, balancing; subsequently joining two, three, four exercises. That would be the easiest way to fall off! No, when a child has a bike for the first time, what do we see? Adults running alongside, holding the saddle, supporting the child no matter how much wobbling occurs in the

The Golden Turtle and Other Tales

process. The child is using ankles, legs, arms and hands to ride the bike shakily until balance, control and confidence are achieved. That's how we all learn new skills: by getting every strategy working in unison from the beginning and refining the details later.

Consider how children learn to talk. On average their increase in two-word utterances ranges from one or two at 18 months to 2,500 at 24 months. Two-word utterances like *mummy car* and *daddy work* say everything they need to express.

Think about the feedback that children receive from their carers who pick up on what children *mean* and not the form in which it's said.

Learning to read

This brings us to reading. Is learning to read somehow different from learning other skills? It is just as holistic an activity as anything else. In order to read fluently you have to co-ordinate a whole range of strategies at the same time. Just like the child careering on the bike or using two-word utterances, you have to get every strategy working in unison from the start. That means having lots of material to practise on at a very basic level.

The Golden Turtle and Other Tales

Children should be seen as readers from the moment they open their first book, or notice an item of junk mail, or see their first advert on television. There is a huge body of evidence which supports the very early development of emergent literacy. Children hypothesise about print as soon as their eyes can focus. So learning to read is a holistic skill too and children entering school, whatever their background experience, have already learnt a great deal about reading and print.

Learning to love reading

Some years ago, a researcher, interviewing children about their reading, asked a seven-year-old boy why he was learning to read at school. "So I can stop," he replied. What this illustrates is that unless we promote positive attitudes to reading at every stage of the learning-to-read process, then we are wasting our time. No one has summed this up better than Margaret Meek (alias Spencer), an eminent commentator on children's books and reading, when she said:

The way children are taught to read tells them what adults think literacy is.

So spend a little time examining what you think literacy is and translate that into your teaching. Does it help you *get away*, enrich your experience, give you pleasure, make you laugh, cry, hope?

Literature in literacy

Two other statements by Margaret Meek are compelling and pertinent:

> *Our most pressing unsolved problem is to define and exemplify the place of children's literature in literacy.*

and

> *What the beginner reader reads makes all the difference to his/her view of reading.*

Today we see more children's books being used alongside reading materials produced especially for the classroom. Such materials have improved enormously, especially in recent years. *Collins Big Cat* is a case in point. It offers books that have the qualities of authorship and illustration of the best children's books on the market, and the kind of readability grading which helps teachers to match books to children's developing competencies, as well as built-in support for key reading strategies.

Readability grading

Over the years there have been various attempts to band, stage or level a wide range of children's books. The first edition of my own *Individualised Reading* appeared in 1973 and was revised annually until 2006. *Book Bands for Guided Reading* (Reading Recovery UK) is the latest established guide to readability grading. The grading used within *Collins Big Cat* refers to *Book Bands*.

What lies behind all these supports for a mix-and-match approach to reading resource provision in schools? It is because this approach leads to greater variety in the books we now find in classrooms – at best a variety which reflects the choice offered in bookshops and libraries. It supports an important principle: that children have ready access to the books they *want* to read, not those they are told they *should* read. This element of choice is vitally important in building children's independent reading habits which, if what's on offer is of sufficient quality, can create lifelong readers.

Great Greek Myths

Book-matching

Book-matching is, simply put, giving the right book to the right child.
It establishes three levels of reading competence to determine which books
should be used for which purposes.

Independent level = 1% miscue* or 99% accuracy
This level is useful for home reading as children can read such
books on their own.

Instructional level = 5–10% miscue or 90–95% accuracy
This level is useful for guided (or supported) reading.

Frustration level = over 10% miscue or less than 90% accuracy
This level should always be avoided (comprehension is below 50%
at this level).

Nightmare: Two Ghostly Tales

Don't forget that when children are particularly interested in a story or
topic, or have seen it on television, their match point can be anything
up to four levels higher than usual. Similarly, for reluctant readers,
allow for a corresponding drop in level.

Research in the early 1990s revealed that one of the characteristics of
successful reading was the classroom provision of slightly challenging
reading material. Switching to the instructional level during guided reading
normally meets the slightly challenging criterion.

Book-matching solves a number of issues, firstly in relation to children who
are expected to read books which they can't manage just on the basis of
their age. Remember that every child has the right to be a reader from the
very start and reading as late as age nine is still in the so-called "normal"
range. It's my belief that no child under this age should ever be labelled
"late", "delayed" or such like.

At the other extreme are children who can read before they start school.
I love the story of the boy who read poetry at 18 months. On being
professionally assessed, he was said to be "unfit to commence reading
instruction". The main reason such children tend to go unrecognised is that
teachers don't expect their proficiency. Expect it. Imagine the effect on the
self-confidence of children who can read but who are nonetheless given
books that are far below their competence. What these children need is
plenty of good books at the right level to interest and challenge them.
Book-matching used correctly should mean that this happens.

*For this purpose, miscues are generally defined as refusals or substitutions which fail to retain the
meaning of the original word.

Collins Big Cat

Collins Big Cat is a reading series with a difference. That difference lies chiefly in the quality and variety of stories and non-fiction books, written and illustrated by carefully selected authors and artists who know what children love. These books are indistinguishable from the books children choose to read in bookshops and libraries, with themes of universal interest for ages four to 11. Moreover, they are levelled into a readability sequence to support teachers working on the book-match principle, whether for guided or independent reading.

Language

We have gone to great lengths, through extensive trialling with children and teachers, to ensure that the language used in every book is as close to a child's natural language as possible, to support their developing confidence in reading. Design and illustration have also been trialled, ensuring that the books build in factors that make the act of reading more accessible and that act as a safeguard against "getting it wrong". In *Moving Out*, a narrative set in post-World-War-II Britain, the language of the *Eagle* comic's hero Dan Dare evokes the sci-fi preoccupations of the period. Similarly, *The Traveller's Guide to the Solar System* is written in a style which looks forward from the present to a time when space travel will be as common as European package holidays are now.

A humorous recount

Story genres

Collins Big Cat provides a full range of reading through different genres, from traditional tales, fantasy and stories set in the past to jokes and humorous stories. And from non-fiction explanations and instructions to recounts and persuasive texts. This range gives children a broad, exciting and enjoyable reading experience throughout the primary years.

Two stories by a significant author

Non-chronological report

Information book

Stories from other cultures

Instruction book

Visual literacy – "filling the gaps"

We have continued to illustrate every book lavishly and we have also ensured that, in many cases, both the text and the pictures must be read in order to gain full meaning from the book. In this way, children are being encouraged to "fill the gaps", a mark of literary awareness. Look, for example, at *Fragile Earth* where pairs of photographs reveal stunning and often alarming comparisons of changing landscapes over relatively short periods of time. These images speak for themselves.

Fragile Earth

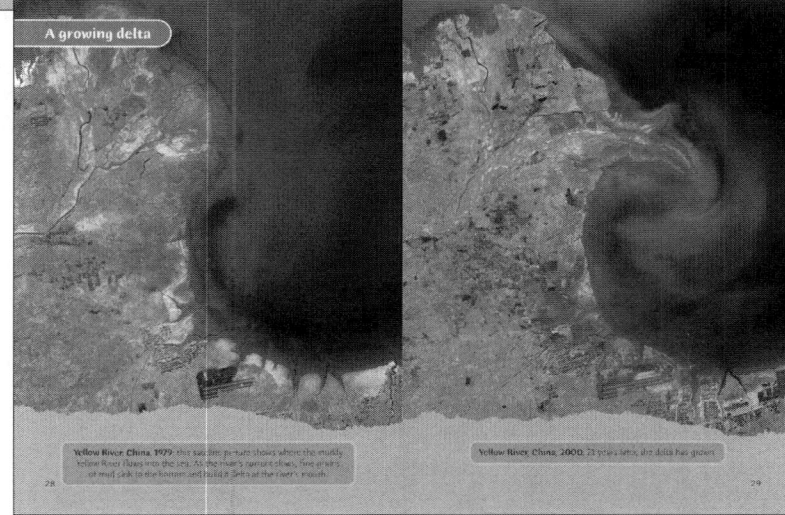

Fragile Earth

Reading more, mini-series and paired books

Ways to encourage children to explore different genres and read more have been built into *Collins Big Cat*. The *Reading more* section of *Ideas for guided reading* at the back of every book, highlights links by theme, topic, author, etc., to books in the same reading band or one higher.

Mini-series occur throughout the scheme with, for example, *How to be a Tudor in 20 easy stages* at Ruby and *How to be an Ancient Greek in 25 easy stages* at Sapphire. There are fiction and non-fiction linked themes running

Moving Out

through the levels. At Sapphire, for instance, *The Ultimate World Quiz* gives an array of fascinating facts about our planet, while *The Golden Turtle and Other Tales* explores different cultures through three stories set in different places around the world. *Moving Out* examines day-to-day life in post-World-War-II Britain for a family in London, and *Hard Times* looks at life as a Victorian.

Hard Times

Reading response activity

Collins Big Cat books, fiction and non-fiction, include a unique reading response activity at the end, for example, a story map, a newspaper article, a storyboard, a map or a poster. This has been designed to elicit and encourage the child's response to, and recall understanding of, what he or she has read. These pages offer an ideal opportunity to monitor children's understanding of the book just read.

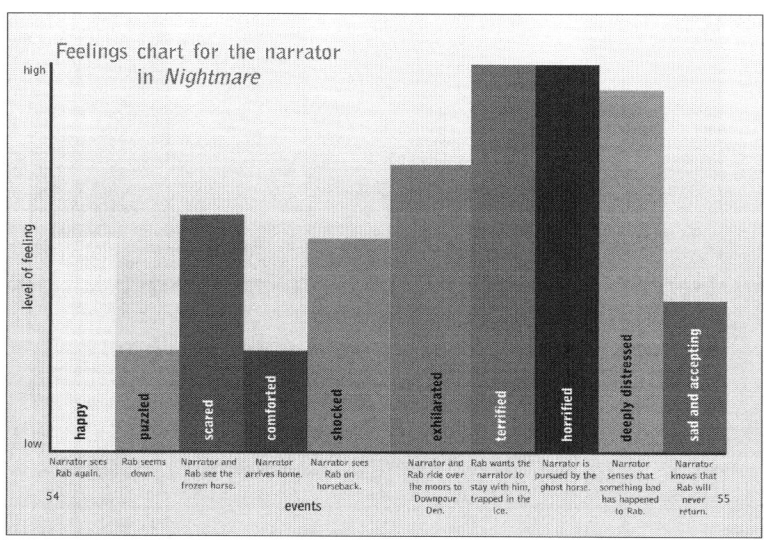

Nightmare: Two Ghostly Tales

Readability

Within *Collins Big Cat*, care has been taken wherever possible to incorporate factors within the design which support the text's readability for children. Examples include:

- no sentences are split by page breaks
- avoidance of short lines of text which could be easily "missed"
- a variety of suitable fonts at all levels so that children encounter print in different forms
- extensive use of ellipses (...) to encourage anticipation and prediction (children love them!).

A vital consideration in *Collins Big Cat* books for nine–11 year olds is their readability gradings, which follow this pattern:

Band	Approximate age	Year/Scottish Year	National Curriculum level
Sapphire	nine to ten	5/P6	Working towards 4
Diamond	ten to 11	6/P7	Working within 4

And finally ...

Take a look at *The Golden Turtle and Other Tales*, a trio of stories from world cultures by Gervase Phinn – "the James Herriot of northern primary schools". The first is set in Japan, the second in Spain and the third in Ireland. In each the illustrations reflect locations and themes extremely sensitively. Similarly, *Hard Times* gives children another cultural perspective in the examination of the working lives of children in the Victorian era through engravings, photos and paintings of the time. The book culminates in a section showing children who have to work to survive in today's world.

The Golden Turtle and Other Tales

a mudlark

a child scavenging on a rubbish dump

Hard Times

How to use this guide

Collins Big Cat Assessment and Support Guides provide teachers with practical planning and teaching support, helping them to assess and identify the needs of each child or group, and to teach essential literacy skills in the context of guided reading.

This guide has five main sections:

A Letter from Cliff Moon – pages 4 to 11

Collins Big Cat series editor Cliff Moon introduces *Collins Big Cat* and explains why it is such a boon to children's reading.

Structure and features – pages 14 to 19

This section outlines the content and structure of *Collins Big Cat*, including an overview of where to find what, a structure chart and further resources.

Planning and teaching – pages 18 to 33

These pages are a practical planning tool designed to help you identify quickly the right book for your guided reading groups. They provide an at-a-glance synopsis of the features of each book, including interest words, key learning objectives, supporting materials and curriculum links. In addition, easy-to-use two-page teaching notes giving a sample guided reading lesson are provided in the back of each *Collins Big Cat* reading book. There are also detailed links to the Scottish Curriculum for Excellence.

Photocopiable activity sheets – pages 34 to 49

There is a photocopiable activity sheet to accompany each of the guided reading books. These can be used to practise and extend the literacy objectives introduced in the guided reading lesson.

Collins Big Cat and guided reading – pages 50 to 57

This section provides further information on the key features of guided reading and its use within a balanced literacy programme. It also offers support in using effective assessment techniques and ideas to encourage the development of independent reading habits, for example, reading journals. There is also a full colour guide to guided reading book bands Copper to Diamond on the inside back cover.

 If you feel confident about using guided readers with your children, you could go straight to the teaching summaries on page 18.

 To learn more about *Collins Big Cat* and why it encourages the development of successful young readers, go to page 4.

 For an in-depth discussion of guided reading from ages nine to 11, turn to page 50.

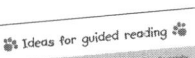

 To look at a range of assessment techniques to help you identify the needs of individuals or groups, turn to page 56.

Features of *Collins Big Cat* Guided Reading Books

Collins Big Cat offers exciting reads designed to capture children's imagination, entertain them and encourage them to love reading. As children read *Collins Big Cat* books, they will benefit from the following features:

Wide range of genres

Collins Big Cat offers an equal split between fiction and non-fiction books and a wide variety of genres and text types – e.g. humorous stories, traditional stories, rhyming stories, non-chronological reports and recounts. At each level is a pair of fiction and non-fiction books on related themes, enabling teachers to link easily across genres.

Top authors

The books – fiction and non-fiction – are written by a range of outstanding children's authors. These include Michael Morpurgo, Berlie Doherty, Geraldine McCaughrean, Julia Donaldson, Nick Butterworth, Ian Whybrow, Alan Durant, Michael Rosen, Martin Waddell, Tony Mitton and Ros Asquith. Top quality texts make reading enjoyable for a child, which is a huge stimulus to learning.

Trixie Tempest's Diary

VERY EXTREMELY BORING DIARY YOU'RE WELCOME TO READ IT

Hah! I've called this diary BORING to stop nosey parkers trying to get their hands on it.

Trixie's tip: Never write "TOP SECRET" or "PARENTS KEEP OUT" because everyone will try to have a peek.

straw bunches

happy smile

Write in this Diary EVERY DAY!!

 ABOUT ME

Name: Trixie Tempest

School: St Aubergine's Primary

Hair: Straw mat. I keep it in bunches. I did it up in beads once for World Bead Day or something, but they all fell out in assembly. Ping ping pingetty ping.

Teeth: One stupid baby tooth in front, which looks like a polar bear cub standing among a lot of icebergs.

Face: Freckles with bits of skin in-between. Thank goodness for skin, I say. Without it, we'd all fall out.

Size: I'm the smallest and thinnest in my class so I look like a twig in a jungle.

2

3

Rich illustrations

Collins Big Cat books are illustrated by leading children's illustrators, including Michael Foreman, Satoshi Kitamura, Nick Butterworth, Shoo Rayner, Julian Mosedale, Tony Ross and outstanding photographers such as Nic Bishop and Jonathan and Angela Scott. Each book is highly visual, with pictures that can be used to develop visual literacy and oral retelling.

Speaking and listening

Collins Big Cat has been specifically developed to encourage children's speaking and listening skills as well as their reading skills, by including strong visual plots in the stories and presenting information in a variety of forms in the non-fiction.

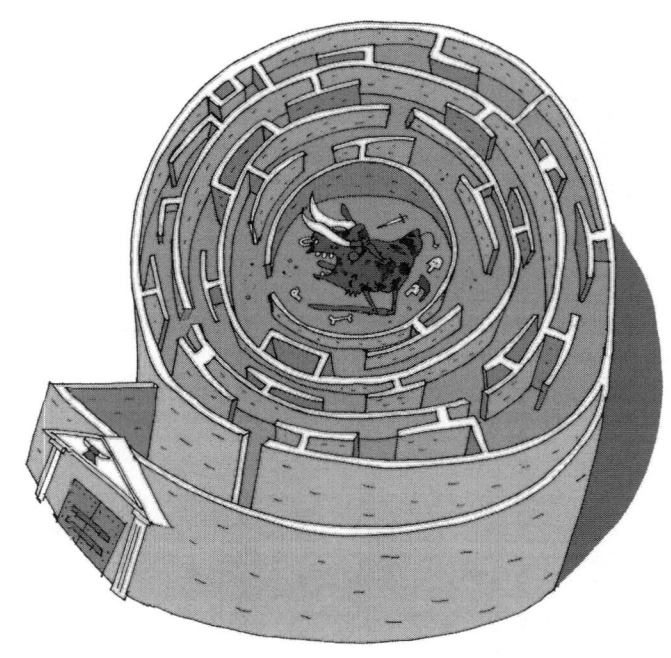

Great Greek Myths

Non-fiction includes diagrams, fact boxes and maps to assist explanation.

Longer, more complex sentences may include some specialist vocabulary.

Where is the longest wall in the world?

Can you imagine a wall so long that it would stretch from London in the UK to Chicago in the USA? Well, the *Great Wall of China* is just such a wall. It stretches about 6,400 kilometres through the mountains and deserts of northern China. It's the longest wall in the world.

Did you know?
It's often said that the Great Wall of China can be seen from the Moon. This is untrue, although the Wall can be seen by satellites far above the Earth.

The enormous structure was built by slaves. Work on it began over 2,200 years ago by order of the first Chinese emperor, Shi Huangdi. He hoped that the Wall would keep out invaders who threatened China from the north. Later emperors continued the work on the Wall. In truth, it's not one single wall, but a number of different walls joined together. Along its length are 25,000 square watchtowers. These were manned by Chinese guards, who watched the desolate hills for signs of danger. Signals were sent to warn of an attack – either by smoke, during the day, or by fire, at night.

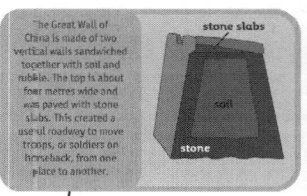

The Great Wall of China is made of two vertical walls sandwiched together with soil and rubble. The top is about four metres wide and was paved with stone slabs. This created a useful roadway to move troops, or soldiers on horseback, from one place to another.

Did you know?
Each year, a marathon is held along the Great Wall of China. With its steep climbs and stairways, the wall is a gruelling challenge for athletes.

The Ultimate World Quiz

Text and pictures are laid out in a variety of ways. Pictures support the meaning of the text.

Reading response activity

Each book has a unique reading response activity at the end of it. This enables you to check each child's comprehension through speaking and listening in response to the spread. The wide range of activities, from storyboards to flow charts to maps to newspaper articles, are ideal supports for recapping, retelling and revisiting the main events in the book, as well as linking to activity work outside the guided session.

Selim-Hassan the Seventh and The Wall

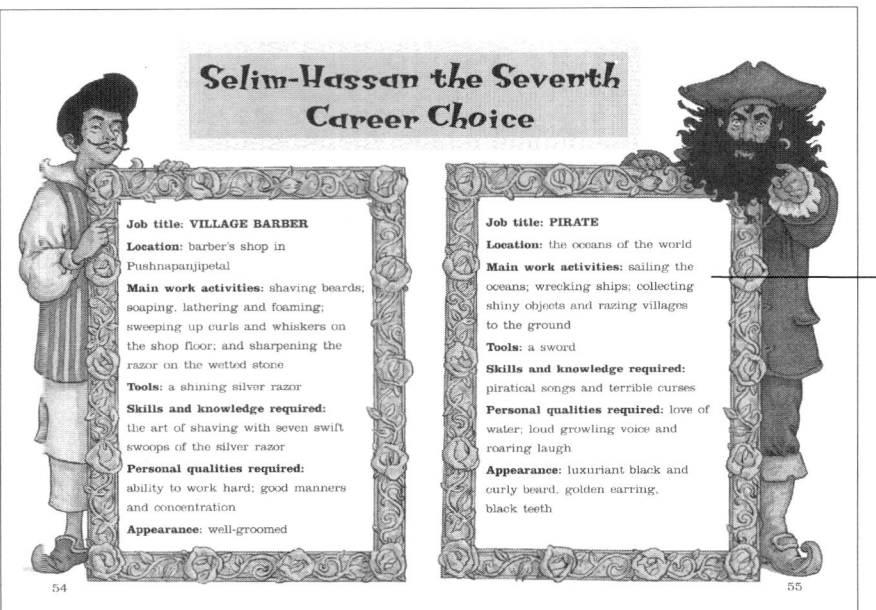

These career profiles prompt children to express opinions about the choices made in the book and consider the consequences of actions.

Collins Big Cat book bands

Collins Big Cat is clearly structured into bands based on the Institute of Education's *Guided Reading Book Bands*, and is both easy to use as a core programme, or alongside existing resources for guided reading. For more information on the Copper–Diamond bands, turn to the colour chart on the inside back cover.

Colour-coded bands help you match Big Cat to the children's ability level.

Ideas for guided reading at your fingertips

At the back of every *Collins Big Cat* guided reading book is a double-page spread of *Ideas for guided reading*. These are provided in every *Collins Big Cat* book so they are right at your fingertips during guided reading lessons. *Ideas for guided reading* give you a range of useful information as well as outlining the most effective way to use the book in a guided reading session.

Learning objectives
Helps you plan learning objectives, based on PNS Framework objectives.

Curriculum links
Enables you to link the reading to other areas of the school curriculum.

Interest words
Gives you, at a glance, the interest words children will tackle when reading this book.

Returning to the book
Recapping and reviewing the text and learning objectives, with support of the reading response activity at the end of the book.

Great Greek Myths

:paw: Ideas for guided reading :paw:

Learning objectives: compare different types of narrative and information texts and identify how they are structured; infer writers' perspectives from what is written and what is implied; explore how writers use language for comic and dramatic effects; use and explore different question types

Curriculum links: History: Who were the Ancient Greeks?, How do we use Ancient Greek ideas today?

Interest words: labours, mortal, oracle, arrowhead, marathon, hydra, minotaur, Hades, underworld, Cerberus

Resources: question cards: Who? What? Why? Where? When? How?, picture of the hydra and the minotaur

Getting started

This book can be read over two or more guided reading sessions.

- Read the title and blurb on the front and back covers. Ask if anyone knows any characters from the Greek myths. Introduce the hydra and the minotaur as examples.
- Discuss and explain what the word "myth" means.
- Read the contents together. Model and remind children to use a range of strategies to read new and tricky words.
- Explain that you are going to read about the labours of Herakles. Ask children to predict what a "labour" might be.

Reading and responding

- Read pp2-3 to the children. Discuss the tone of the narrative voice. Is it funny or serious? Formal or informal? Approving or disapproving of Herakles? Ask children to give reasons for their ideas.
- In pairs, ask children to read to p10 to find out how Herakles defeats the lion of Nemea. Discuss the narrative voice and ask for examples of humour and dramatic language.

- Divide children up so that they each read about one of the following labours: the hydra (pp10-13), the stinking stables (pp14-17), the minotaur (pp18-20), the flesh-eating mares (pp22-24) the golden apples (pp25-28) and Cerberus (pp28-31).

Returning to the book

- Ask children to recount their labour to the group using dramatic language. Have a competition to see who can be the most dramatic.
- Debate which labour was the most dangerous. Help children to support their ideas by referring to the stories.
- In pairs, ask children to read the interview on pp54-55 aloud, taking the roles of JRD and Herakles.

Checking and moving on

- In pairs, plan to interview King Eurystheus for his side of the story. Plan a set of questions and create question cards as prompts.
- Hot seat children as King Eurystheus using the question cards.
- Read the other myths in the book and research Greek myths using the Internet.
- Make fact files for the mythical beasts included in the stories.

HYDRA	MINOTAUR	CERBERUS
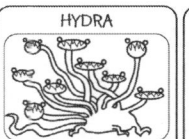		
• nine-headed, man-eating monster • blazing eyes and spitting tongues • lives on the coastland	• gigantic Cretan bull • razor-tipped horns • lives in a maze	• three-headed hound of hell • sharp, vicious teeth • guards the gates of Hades

Reading more

How to be an Ancient Greek (Sapphire/Band 16) is an information book about the Ancient Greeks.

Getting started
Ideas and activities to introduce the book and learning objectives.

Reading and responding
Ideas to support the group's independent reading of the book, prompting the children to problem solve as they read and to predict what might happen next.

Checking and moving on
Ideas and activities for group, paired or independent work arising from the guided reading.

Reading more
This suggests another book the children can read at the same or next reading level, related by subject, author or genre.

At-a-glance information to help teachers plan their guided reading lesson.

Collins Big Cat Sapphire and Diamond books

This guide contains book-by-book details and planning notes for all *Collins Big Cat* guided reading books from book bands Sapphire and Diamond.

The chart opposite directs you to the right page for information and PCMs for all the Sapphire and Diamond guided reading books. To find a short text summary, learning objectives, interest words and related resources for a particular guided reading book, look at the page number next to "Info". To find the PCM for the particular book, look at the number next to "PCM". The PCMs are numbered 1 to 16 and they start on page 34.

Fiction

Sapphire / Band 16

Great Greek Myths

Fiction

Info **20**

PCM **1**

Three traditional tales

The Monkey Puppet

Fiction

Info **20**

PCM **2**

A mystery story

Trixie Tempest's Diary

Fiction

Info **20**

PCM **3**

A humorous recount

Diamond / Band 17

Selim-Hassan the Seventh and The Wall

Fiction

Info **24**

PCM **9**

Two stories from other cultures

Fearless Flynn and other tales

Fiction

Info **26**

PCM **10**

Three fantasy stories

Nightmare: Two Ghostly Tales

Fiction

Info **26**

PCM **11**

Two stories by a significant author

Fiction/non-fiction topic-linked		Non-fiction		

The Golden Turtle and Other Tales

Fiction

Info **22**

PCM **4**

Three stories from other cultures

The Ultimate World Quiz

Non-fiction

Info **22**

PCM **5**

An information book

How to be an Ancient Greek

Non-fiction

Info **22**

PCM **6**

An information book

The Traveller's Guide to the Solar System

Non-fiction

Info **24**

PCM **7**

A non-chronological report

Michael Rosen: All About Me

Non-fiction

Info **24**

PCM **8**

An autobiography

Moving Out

Fiction

Info **26**

PCM **12**

A story set in the past

Hard Times

Non-fiction

Info **28**

PCM **13**

A non-chronological report

Fragile Earth

Non-fiction

Info **28**

PCM **14**

A non-chronological report

How to Make Manga Characters

Non-fiction

Info **28**

PCM **15**

An instruction book

Designing Places and Spaces

Non-fiction

Info **30**

PCM **16**

An information book

Book band	About the book		Text type	Curriculum links

Sapphire / Band 16

Great Greek Myths

Diane Redmond and Julian Mosedale

Three well-known Greek myths are humorously recounted in this book of traditional tales. Herakles has to show great bravery, strength and courage to overcome the challenges he is set; Theseus kills the minotaur with the help of a cunning idea; and Daedalus and Icarus have a clever plan to escape the maze where they are imprisoned. Children can explore how the narrative voice is designed to make the book appealing by considering how humour and drama are injected into each story. The magazine interview with Herakles on pages 54 and 55 offers a modern approach to an age-old tale.

Three traditional tales

History: Who were the Ancient Greeks?, How do we use Ancient Greek ideas today?

Sapphire / Band 16

The Monkey Puppet

Leon Rosselson and James de la Rue

This mystery story begins with a familiar school setting, but it is soon clear that there is something strange about the new boy, Mark, who will only speak through his monkey puppet. When Daniel is asked to look after him, he is unsure, but he has no idea how dangerous things will become. This suspense-filled story will help children to reflect on how the author is arousing feelings of empathy, as well as using techniques to create dramatic effects. The story cards provided on pages 54 and 55 can be used to explore how authors structure and use settings to create suspense within mystery stories.

A mystery story

Citizenship: Taking part – developing skills of communication and participation, Moving on

---

Sapphire / Band 16

Trixie Tempest's Diary

Ros Asquith

In this wickedly funny diary, the reader meets Trixie Tempest, and learns about her friends, family, school-life and pet dogs, Harpo and Bonzo. Trixie uses her diary to recount information and plan a variety of projects that will improve the world. A range of writing styles and vibrant illustrations are used to engage the reader and can act as models for a variety of children's own writing. Bonzo's Doggy Diary on pages 54 and 55 will help readers to recount events from the story and develop their understanding of writing from different perspectives.

A humorous recount

Citizenship: Animals and us, Developing our school grounds

Learning objectives	Interest words	Related resources
Primary Framework objectives Year 5 Speaking: Use and explore different question types and different ways words are used, including in formal and informal contexts. Understanding and interpreting texts: Compare different types of narrative and information texts and identify how they are structured; Infer writers' perspectives from what is written and what is implied; Explore how writers use language for comic and dramatic effects. Scottish Curriculum for Excellence: Listening and Talking, Reading, Writing, Second Stage	labours, mortal, oracle, arrowhead, marathon, hydra, minotaur, Hades, underworld, Cerberus	**PCM 1:** Children are asked to design a fact file for a new creature.
Primary Framework objectives Year 5 Drama: Reflect on how working in role helps to explore complex issues. Understanding and interpreting texts: Compare different types of narrative and information texts and identify how they are structured; Explore how writers use language for comic and dramatic effects. Engaging with and responding to texts: Compare the usefulness of techniques such as visualisation, prediction and empathy in exploring the meaning of texts. Scottish Curriculum for Excellence: Listening and Talking, Reading, Writing, Second Stage	conceited, confiscate, sinister, concocting, ventriloquist, intervened, silhouetted, mesmerised, evading	**PCM 2:** Children are asked to record the thoughts of Mark and Daniel.
Primary Framework objectives Year 5 Speaking: Present a spoken argument, sequencing points logically, defending views and making use of persuasive language. Understanding and interpreting texts: Infer writer's perspective from what is written and what is implied; Explore how writers use language for comic and dramatic effects Scottish Curriculum for Excellence: Listening and Talking, Reading, Writing, Second Stage	ventriloquist, campaigned, fiends, wheezing, severed, collided, confession, contracted	**PCM 3:** Children complete an About Me profile for one of the other characters in the book.

Book band	About the book	Text type	Curriculum links

Sapphire / Band 16

The Golden Turtle and Other Tales

Gervase Phinn and Linda Selby, Tomislav Zlatic and Sholto Walker

In these three entertaining folk tales from around the world, characters encounter a range of testing challenges and events. A poor fisherman must decide what to do when he catches a valuable golden turtle; Amparo, a little Spanish girl with a fierce spirit, must overcome great danger to find a way for her and her brothers to pay their debts; a naughty leprechaun causes mischief wherever he goes, but learns a valuable lesson when he finds himself without any friends when he needs them most. A "Wanted" poster on pages 54 and 55 supports children as they develop the ability to recount key events and information from each story. This title is paired with *The Ultimate World Quiz* by Claire Llewellyn.

Three stories from other cultures

Geography: Passport to the world; Citizenship: Choices, Living in a diverse world

---

Sapphire / Band 16

The Ultimate World Quiz

Claire Llewellyn

This stunning information book is full of fascinating facts about the world and is structured using a range of questions that will interest and provoke discussion. Written information is supported with stunning photography, illustrations and *Did you know?* boxes to give further meaning and raise additional questions. Contents are organised by continent, so children will develop their geographical knowledge as they read from each section. On pages 54 and 55, a world map shows the places described in the book and helps children to recall and review their reading. The glossary and index on pages 52 and 53 allow children to use retrieval devices to practise locating and appraising information quickly and effectively. This title is paired with *The Golden Turtle and Other Tales* by Gervase Phinn.

An information book

Geography: Passport to the world

Sapphire / Band 16

How to be an Ancient Greek

Scoular Anderson

In this humorous and entertaining book, topics range from the extreme sports that the Ancient Greeks enjoyed to the legacy of the Ancient Greeks found in our language today. The information is presented clearly, using labelled diagrams and lively, fun illustrations to support a range of readers. The book also includes the full range of retrieval devices (contents, index and glossary) to support children as they learn to search for, and locate, information.

An information book

History: Who were the Ancient Greeks?, How do we use Ancient Greek ideas today?

Learning objectives	Interest words	Related resources
Primary Framework objectives Year 5 Speaking: Tell a story using notes designed to cue techniques, such as repetition, recap and humour. Understanding and interpreting texts: Compare different types of narrative and information texts and identify how they are structured; Explore how writers use language for comic and dramatic effects. Scottish Curriculum for Excellence: Listening and Talking, Reading, Writing, Second Stage	folk tale, Oranmore, leprechaun, mischievous, billowing, whimpered	**PCM 4:** Children complete a planning chart for retelling a folk tale.
Primary Framework objectives Year 5 Speaking: Use and explore different question types and different ways words are used, including in formal and informal contexts. Understanding and interpreting texts: Make notes on and use evidence across a text to explain events or ideas; Compare different types of narrative and information texts and identify how they are structured. Scottish Curriculum for Excellence: Listening and Talking, Reading, Writing, Second Stage	arid, canopy, headland, migrate, molten, plains, probes	**PCM 5:** A template for a true or false quiz for children to create for friends or family.
Primary Framework objectives Year 5 Drama: Use and recognise the impact of theatrical effects in drama. Understanding and interpreting texts: Make notes on and use evidence from across a text to explain events or ideas; Compare different types of information texts and identify how they are structured. Scottish Curriculum for Excellence: Listening and Talking, Reading, Writing, Second Stage	besieged, feat, fortified, frieze, migrated, pediment, recite, sacred	**PCM 6:** A comparison chart template for children to note the differences between life in Ancient Greek times and life today.

Book band	About the book		Text type	Curriculum links

Sapphire / Band 16

The Traveller's Guide to the Solar System

Giles Sparrow

Readers are transported to the Solar System as they become holiday-makers in outer space. Having considered health and safety and travel options, readers visit different planets, comets and asteroids to learn about each planet and its associated phenomena. Amazing illustrations and *Did you know?* boxes support the written information. Children can be encouraged to raise questions prior to reading to support information retrieval. As each planet is reported in turn, children can research and debate where they would like to travel to and why. The Solar System must-sees chart on pages 54 and 55 can be used to stimulate this discussion.	A non-chronological report

Curriculum links: Science: Earth, Sun, and Moon

Sapphire / Band 16

Michael Rosen: All About Me

Michael Rosen

This fascinating autobiography introduces Michael Rosen to his young audience and reveals facts from different stages in his life that have inspired his career as a poet and writer. Beautifully illustrated with line drawings as well as photographs and archive material, this book will inspire young readers to consider their own histories as well as Michael Rosen's. An index and glossary are included to support information retrieval and comprehension, while the timeline on pages 54 and 55 can be used to support readers as they research Rosen's life further.

Text type: An autobiography

Curriculum links: History: What can we learn about recent history from studying the life of a famous person?

Diamond / Band 17

Selim-Hassan the Seventh and The Wall

Vivian French and Tim Stevens

Two magical tales from far-off lands are recounted in these exotic stories. Through an unpleasant encounter, Selim-Hassan learns to value his father's work and profession, while Little Rabbit shows the true bravery and spirit of a daughter and granddaughter as she climbs the Great Wall of China to return her grandmother to her birthplace. These tales are recounted from the third and first person and provide the opportunity to explore different ways of structuring and retelling stories. A career choice chart for Selim-Hassan on pages 54 and 55 can be used to stimulate debate and discussion.

Text type: Two stories from other cultures

Curriculum links: Geography: Passport to the world; Citizenship: Living in a diverse world

Learning objectives	Interest words	Related resources
Primary Framework objectives Year 5 Group discussion and interaction: Plan and manage a group task over time using different levels of planning. Understanding and interpreting texts: Make notes on and use evidence from across a text to explain events or ideas. Engaging with and responding to texts: Reflect on reading habits and preferences and plan personal reading goals. Scottish Curriculum for Excellence: Listening and Talking, Reading, Writing, Second Stage	asteroids, atmosphere, gravity, meteorite, orbit, protoplanets, satellite, Solar System, supernova	**PCM 7:** A fact file template for children to complete for one of the Solar System destinations.
Primary Framework objectives Year 5 Group discussion and interaction: Plan and manage a group task over time using different levels of planning. Understanding and interpreting texts: Make notes on and use evidence from across a text to explain events or ideas; Infer writers' perspectives from what is written and what is implied. Engaging and responding to texts: Reflect on reading habits and preferences and plan personal reading goals. Scottish Curriculum for Excellence: Listening and Talking, Reading, Writing, Second Stage	Biology, charades, dissecting, documentaries, Laureate, meningitis, spectrometer, splayed, suburb, Yiddish	**PCM 8:** Children complete a personal timeline.
Primary Framework objectives Year 6 Speaking: Use the techniques of dialogic talk to explore ideas, topics or issues. Understanding and interpreting texts: Understand how writers use different structures to create coherence and impact. Engaging with and responding to texts: Sustain engagement with longer texts, using different techniques to make the text come alive. Scottish Curriculum for Excellence: Listening and Talking, Reading, Writing, Second Stage	luxuriant, piratical, illustrious, ancestor, monstrous, barricade, tedious	**PCM 9:** A storyboard template for children to record the key moments of one of the stories.

Book band	About the book		Text type	Curriculum links

Diamond / Band 17

Fearless Flynn and other tales

Gillian Shields, Geraldine McCaughrean and Martin Waddell

Three spooky stories are dramatically retold in this suspense-filled chapter book. Fearless Flynn battles with skeletons; Tom is changed forever by witnessing something very strange at night; and thirteen crows bring disaster wherever they are sighted. Children will enjoy recounting these and other spooky tales as they explore the different structures and features used by authors as they create suspense in their stories. Each tale is structured using chapters or repetition which will help young readers to plot the stories visually and experiment with recounting them orally. A newspaper recount section on pages 54 and 55 models how stories can be interpreted in different ways.

Three fantasy stories

Music: Stars, hide your fires – Performing together

Diamond / Band 17

Nightmare: Two Ghostly Tales

Berlie Doherty

Two spooky stories by award-winning children's author Berlie Doherty are included in this gripping chapter book . Both tales are told from a different central character's point of view and include events that will intrigue and surprise young readers. Discussion is promoted by the mysterious happenings, and readers will develop their skills of inference and deduction as they make meaning. A feelings chart on pages 54 and 55 can be used to recount key events and stimulate drama activities.

Two stories by a significant author

Citizenship: Living in a diverse world

Diamond / Band 17

Moving Out

Sally Prue and Martin Remphry

It is post-war Britain and Philip's family has to decide whether to leave London for a New Town or not. Philip finds himself in the middle of this dilemma: his nan wants to stay in London, and his parents want to leave for a new beginning. Children will see both sides of the argument as they read about Philip's adventures. Reasons for staying and going are presented on pages 54 and 55 and readers can use this resource to support discussion and debate. As well as being historically accurate and informative, this chapter book will support the reading skills of inference and deduction as readers understand each character's motives and attitudes to moving. This title is paired with *Hard Times* by Jillian Powell.

A story set in the past

History: How life in Britain has changed since 1948; Citizenship: Moving on, Choices

Learning objectives	Interest words	Related resources
Primary Framework objectives Year 6 Drama: Devise a performance considering how to adapt the performance for a specific audience. Understanding and interpreting texts: Understand how writers use different structures to create coherence and impact. Engaging with and responding to texts: Sustain engagement with longer texts, using different techniques to make the text come alive. Scottish Curriculum for Excellence: Listening and Talking, Reading, Writing, Second Stage	ambusher, xylophone, toboggan	**PCM 10:** Children are asked to record the thoughts of each of the three skeletons when they meet Fearless Flynn.
Primary Framework objectives Year 6 Speaking: Use a range of oral techniques to present engaging narratives. Understanding and interpreting texts: Understand underlying themes, causes and points of view. Engaging and responding to texts: Sustain engagement with longer texts, using different techniques to make the text come alive. Scottish Curriculum for Excellence: Listening and Talking, Reading, Writing, Second Stage	desolate, fossilised, clamour, shards, sinewy, languorous	**PCM 11:** Children record the key moments of one of the stories.
Primary Framework objectives Year 6 Speaking: Use a range of oral techniques to present persuasive arguments and engaging narratives. Understanding and interpreting texts: Understand underlying themes, causes and points of view. Engaging with and responding to texts: Sustain engagement with longer texts, using different techniques to make the text come alive. Scottish Curriculum for Excellence: Listening and Talking, Reading, Writing, Second Stage	blitz, dilemma, indignantly, experimentally, pointedly, loyally, newfangled, grudgingly	**PCM 12:** Children record the key moments in one of the stories.

Book band	About the book	Text type	Curriculum links

Diamond / Band 17

Hard Times

Jillian Powell

Readers find out what life was like in Victorian times for poor and rich children as they read this fascinating report. Chapters cover a wide range of appealing topics, including the schooling and clothes that Victorian children had and, in the final chapter, connections are made with today's children's lives which encourage further research. Stunning photographs and fact boxes are used to illustrate the information that is being presented and support readers' comprehension and questioning skills. Contents, glossary and index pages are included to aid information retrieval skills, and a key dates section on pages 54 and 55 can be used to encourage further skimming and scanning of the text. This title is paired with *Moving Out* by Sally Prue.

Text type: A non-chronological report

Curriculum links: History: What was it like for children living in Victorian Britain?

Fragile Earth

Claire Llewellyn

This visually stunning book shows, through a collection of dramatic images, how the natural world is changing around us. Photographs and illustrations provide evidence of the impact and damage that volcanoes, earthquakes and extreme weather can cause. The book will encourage discussion about current issues such as climate change, and allow children to present their own ideas about the topics included. Children will need to consider how fairly the information is reported and the perspective from which the facts are recounted. A review section and map on pages 54 and 55 will help children to locate the events reported and support further research. This information book includes contents, index and glossary to support information retrieval skills.

Text type: A non-chronological report

Curriculum links: Geography: Passport to the world

How to Make Manga Characters

Katy Coope

In this vibrant instruction book, Katy Coope provides a step-by-step guide to creating manga characters. As well as the detailed, practical instructions and examples, the author provides fascinating background information about what manga is and where it comes from. The instructions are presented through a range of techniques to interest and inform, and evaluation and discussion of this can develop comprehension skills. A mind map for manga is provided on pages 54 and 55, which can be used as a resource to help children plan their own manga story, or as a way of supporting children as they recount their reading.

Text type: An instruction book

Curriculum links: Art and Design: People in action

Learning objectives	Interest words	Related resources
Primary Framework objectives Year 6 Speaking: Use the techniques of dialogic talk to explore ideas, topics or issues. Drama: Improvise using a range of drama strategies and conventions to explore themes such as hopes, fears and desires. Understanding and interpreting texts: Appraise a text quickly, deciding on its value, quality or usefulness. Engaging with and responding to texts: Sustain engagement with longer texts, using different techniques to make the text come alive. Scottish Curriculum for Excellence: Listening and Talking, Reading, Writing, Second Stage	abacus, asthma, Empire, Industrial Revolution, phosphorous, poverty, scullery, sewerage, tuberculosis	**PCM 13:** Children are asked to write a letter as a Victorian child.
Primary Framework objectives Year 6 Speaking: Participate in whole-class debate using the conventions and language of debate, including standard English. Understanding and interpreting texts: Understand underlying themes, causes and points of view. Engaging with and responding to texts: Sustain engagement with longer texts, using different techniques to make the text come alive. Scottish Curriculum for Excellence: Listening and Talking, Reading, Writing, Second Stage	atmosphere, current, debris, disused, erodes, hemisphere, irrigation, lagoon, minerals, molten, reservoir, resources, rotates, satellite, sensor, submerged, surge	**PCM 14:** A key facts record sheet template for children to fill in.
Primary Framework objectives Year 6 Speaking: Use the techniques of dialogic talk to explore ideas, topics or issues. Understanding and interpreting texts: Understand how writers use different structures to create coherence and impact. Engaging with and responding to texts: Sustain engagement with longer texts, using different techniques to make the text come alive. Scottish Curriculum for Excellence: Listening and Talking, Reading, Writing, Second Stage	anime, chibi, gitaigo, mangaka, mecha, ninjas	**PCM 15:** Children are asked to create a character web for one of the manga characters.

Book band	About the book	Text type	Curriculum links

Designing Places and Spaces

Adrian Bradbury

In this visually stunning information book, readers are introduced to the idea that everything around them has been designed for a purpose. From children's toys to the world's most amazing parks, buildings and structures, the process of design is introduced and explained. A comprehensive index and glossary help readers to locate and understand information, while on pages 54 and 55, a visual summary can be used to promote speaking and listening activities and further reading.

An information book

Design and Technology: Shelters

Diamond / Band 17

Learning objectives	Interest words	Related resources
Primary Framework objectives Year 6 Speaking: Use the techniques of dialogic talk to explore ideas, topics or issues. Understanding and interpreting texts: Appraise a text quickly, deciding on its value, quality or usefulness. Engaging and responding to texts: Sustain engagement with longer texts, using different techniques to make the text come alive. Scottish Curriculum for Excellence: Listening and Talking, Reading, Writing, Second Stage	architectural, cityscape, foundations, hi-tech, insulation, mishmash, low-rise, nomadic, suburbs, turbine	**PCM 16:** Children are asked to complete a fact file for one of the designs in the book, or for a design they particularly admire.

Collins Big Cat and the Scottish Curriculum for Excellence

The Sapphire and Diamond book bands of *Collins Big Cat* provide a range of opportunities for teachers to extend pupils' language skills, encourage confidence and make reading and learning a pleasurable experience.

As pupils move through the school they will continue to develop their language skills and should be more independent readers ready to share their ideas, pose questions and discuss texts in more detail.

Collins Big Cat's guided reading approach places the teacher at the heart of the learning process, with a high priority to giving pupils a command of English and the ability to use it appropriately and concisely to convey meanings. This includes having a knowledge about language; listening attentively; talking to the point; reading with understanding; and writing fluently and legibly with accurate spelling and punctuation.

Within *Curriculum for Excellence* literacy is defined as: *the set of skills which allows an individual to engage fully in society and in learning, through the different forms of language, and the range of texts, which society values and finds useful.*

Schools are therefore recommended to use the literacy experiences and outcomes to promote the development of skills in using language, particularly those that are used regularly by everyone in their everyday lives. These include:

- the ability to apply knowledge about language
- the need for young people to communicate effectively – orally and in writing
- the importance of listening and talking
- the importance of effective collaborative working
- the important skills of critical literacy
- the need to read for information and being able to work out what trust should be placed on the information and identify when and how people are aiming to persuade or influence.

Providing such skills will involve the following:

Enjoyment and choice: highlighting the importance of providing opportunities for pupils to make increasingly sophisticated choices;

The tools section includes important skills and knowledge, i.e. reading strategies and spelling;

Finding and using information includes critical literacy skills;

Understanding, analysing and evaluating: encouraging progression in understanding of texts, developing not only literal understanding but also the higher order skills;

Creating texts: describing the kind of opportunities which will help pupils to develop the ability to communicate effectively, for example, by writing clear, well-structured explanations.

The resources at this level help to provide a language environment which stimulates pupils' imaginations and their interest and enjoyment of language in all its aspects. The Ideas for guided reading notes support teachers to capitalize on this by providing detailed planning and delivery ideas including speaking and listening, comprehension and writing activities. The suggested teaching approaches and organisation allows for individual, group and class learning supported throughout by the teacher. This is the key to the whole programme. *Curriculum for Excellence* clearly supports this approach and emphasises that learning is an active process. Teachers and other educators are encouraged to consider the ways in which they use listening, talking, reading and writing for learning in their day to day teaching programmes.

Listening and talking for learning:

- Engage with others in group and class discussions of appropriate complexity
- Learn collaboratively
- Explain their thinking to others
- Explore factors which influence them and persuade them in order to help them think about the reliability of information.

Reading for learning:
- Find, select, sort, summarise and link information from a variety of sources
- Consider the purpose and main concerns in texts, and understand the differences between fact and opinion
- Discuss similarities and differences between texts.

Writing for learning:
- Make notes, develop ideas and acknowledge sources in written work
- Develop and use effective vocabulary
- Create texts – for example, presentations – which will allow learners to persuade/argue/explore ideas.

The non-fiction books provide excellent accessible information for young language learners and give the teacher the opportunity to link to other areas of the curriculum. This in turn will encourage pupils to read more widely and so their writing will develop and become more varied. They will demonstrate that they can write about matters which go beyond their real-life experiences, for a larger number of audiences and purposes and from points of view other than their own, extending their ability to write non-narrative texts such as reports, letters and news items.

The fiction books are of longer length and contain chapters. They are stories that will appeal to pupils at this stage and contain a wide variety of characters, settings and plots which will capture their interest and encourage them to talk about their own experiences, feelings and opinions.

The plays introduce children to the key features of playscripts through original stories, traditional tales and updated fairytales. They provide a wealth of speaking and listening opportunities, both in the guided reading session and in drama activities.

As in the earlier stages, assessment is built in to the programme using the Reading Response pages and the photocopiable Ongoing Record and Reading Skill sheets providing the teacher with an opportunity to note pupils' individual needs.

Collins Big Cat and the Scottish Curriculum for Excellence

Curriculum for Excellence Codes	Sapphire	Diamond
Second Stage	**F/NF**	**F/NF**
Listening and Talking		
Enjoyment and choice LIT 2-01a	•	•
Tools for listening and talking LIT 2-02a	•	•
Finding and using information LIT 2-04a/LIT 2-05a/LIT 2-06a	•	•
Understanding, analysing and evaluating LIT 2-07a/LIT 2-08a	•	•
Creating texts LIT 2-09a/LIT 2-10a	•	•
Reading		
Enjoyment and choice LIT 2-11a	•	•
Tools for reading LIT 2-13a	•	•
Finding and using information LIT 2-14a/LIT 2-15a/LIT 2-16a	•	•
Understanding, analysing and evaluating LIT 2-18a	•	•
Writing		
Enjoyment and choice LIT 2-20a	•	•
Tools for writing LIT 2-21a/LIT 2-22a/LIT 2-23a/LIT 2-24a	•	•
Organising and using information LIT 2-25a/LIT 2-26a	•	•
Creating texts LIT 2-28a/LIT 2-29a	•	•

Name _____

Think of a new creature and design a fact file for it. Draw a picture of your creature, give it a name and describe it.

_____

_____

_____

_____

_____

_____

_____

Great Greek Myths

Learning objective: Adapt non-narrative forms and styles to write fiction or factual texts.

Name _____

Imagine you are Mark. You have just been introduced to the class.
Think about how you feel and write it in the thought bubble.

Now imagine you are Daniel. How do you feel after being introduced to Mark
and asked to look after him at school? Write it in the thought bubble.

Good to meet you!

© HarperCollins*Publishers* 2009.

The Monkey Puppet
Learning objective: Experiment with different narrative form and styles.

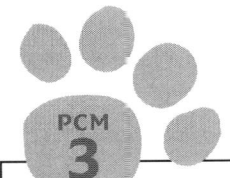

Imagine that you're one of the other characters in the book.
Create an About Me profile like Trixie's, and add a picture for each part.

About Me

Name: _____

_____

_____

_____

_____

_____

_____

_____

_____

_____

_____

_____

_____

_____

_____

_____

Trixie Tempest's Diary
Learning objective: Adapt sentence construction to different text-types, purposes and readers.

Name _____

Fill in this chart to plan how to retell one of the folk tales.

Characters	_____ _____ _____ _____ _____
Key sayings	_____ _____ _____ _____ _____
Key events	_____ _____ _____ _____ _____

The Golden Turtle and Other Tales

Learning objective: Reflect independently and critically on their own writing and edit and improve it.

Name _____

Write a mixture of true and false statements about our planet to test your friends and family.

True or False?

_____ True False
_____ □ □

_____ True False
_____ □ □

_____ True False
_____ □ □

_____ True False
_____ □ □

_____ True False
_____ □ □

_____ True False
_____ □ □

_____ True False
_____ □ □

The Ultimate World Quiz
Learning objective: Adapt sentence construction to different text-types, purposes and readers.

Name _____

Fill in the comparison chart by writing down what is different about life in Ancient Greece and life today in the columns below. Write in complete sentences.

Life in Ancient Greece

Life today

How to be an Ancient Greek
Learning objective: Punctuate sentences accurately.

© HarperCollins*Publishers* 2009.
This page may be photocopied for use in the classroom.

Name _____

Collins
Big Cat

Choose one of the destinations in the Solar System and create a fact file for travellers who are thinking of going there. Draw a picture of your destination in the box.

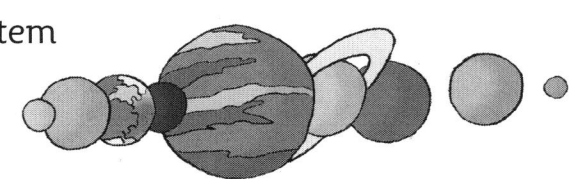

Solar System fact file

Name of destination: _____

Why you should visit: _____

_____

_____

_____

What you need to bring: _____

_____

_____

_____

How long the journey will take: _____

What to be aware of: _____

_____

_____

_____

_____

The Traveller's Guide to the Solar System
Learning objective: Adapt non-narrative forms and styles to write fiction or factual texts.

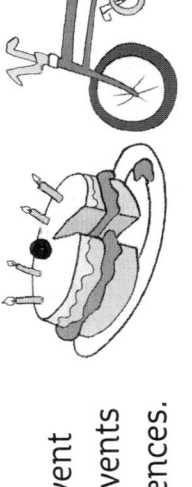

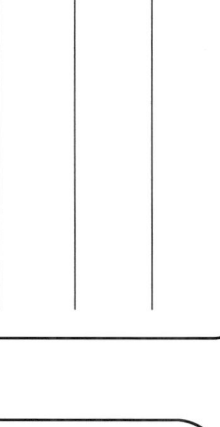

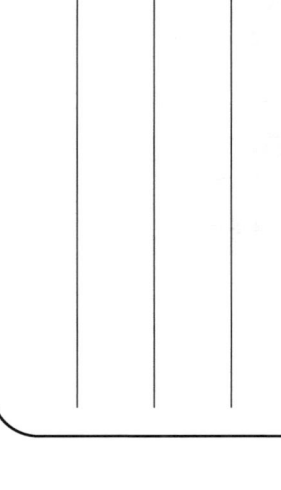

Name _____

Use the timeline to record key events from your life. The first event should be your birth. Think of special, exciting or memorable events that you want to include. Remember to write in complete sentences.

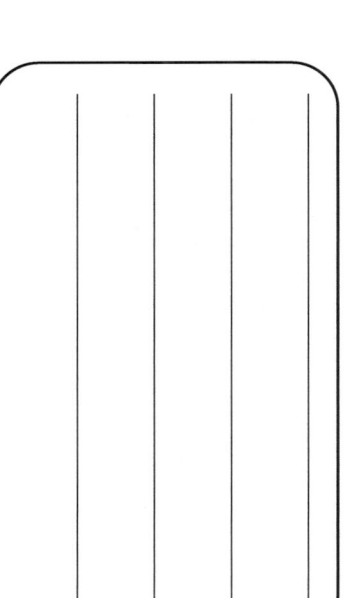

Michael Rosen: All About Me
Learning objective: Punctuate sentences correctly.

© HarperCollins*Publishers* 2009.
This page may be photocopied for use in the classroom.

PCM 8

Collins Big Cat

Name _____

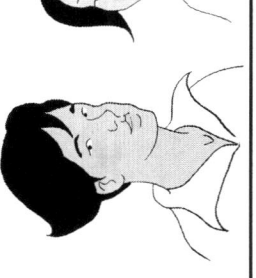

Choose either *Selim-Hassan the Seventh* or *The Wall* and create a storyboard to tell the story. Decide which are the three key moments in the story and draw a picture for each one. Write a caption underneath each picture to explain what happens.

Selim-Hassan the Seventh and The Wall
Learning objective: Integrate words and images imaginatively for different purposes.

PCM
9

Name _____

Imagine you are each of the skeletons. Write down what you are thinking in the thought bubbles as you meet Fearless Flynn.

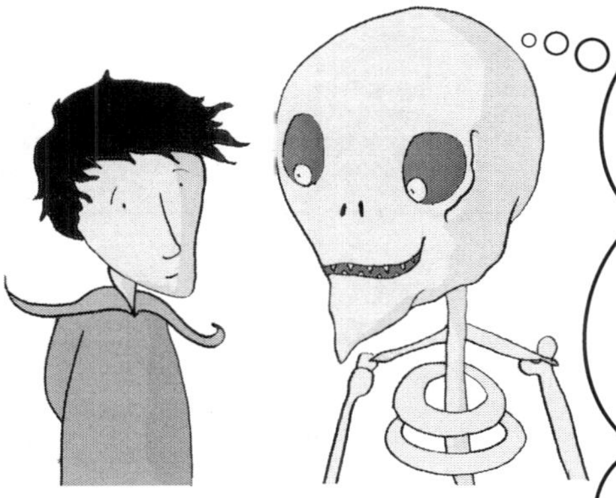

Fearless Flynn and other tales
Learning objective: Use different narrative techniques to engage and entertain the reader.

Name _____

Choose one of the stories from the book. Write the title of your chosen story.
Decide which are the three key moments in the story.
Fill in this chart, remembering to write in full sentences.

Story title: _____

Key moment 1	
Key moment 2	
Key moment 3	

Nightmare: Two Ghostly Tales
Learning objective: Use varied structures to shape and organise text coherently.

Name _____

Imagine you are Philip and you have just been to
the New Town which you're supposed to be moving to.
Fill in this diary entry explaining where you were,
what you saw and how you felt.

Sunday 14th October

_____

_____

_____

_____

_____

_____

_____

_____

_____

_____

_____

Moving Out
Learning objective: Express subtle distinctions of meaning by constructing sentences in varied ways.

Name _____

Imagine you are a Victorian child. Write a letter to
your friend describing what you have done this week.

Dear _____

_____

_____

_____

_____

_____

_____

_____

_____

_____

_____

_____

_____

_____

_____

_____

Hard Times
Learning objective: Select words and language drawing on their knowledge of
literary features and formal and informal writing.
© HarperCollins*Publishers* 2009. This page may be photocopied for use in the classroom.

Name _____

Choose a topic which you are interested in
and fill in this record sheet with the key facts.

47

Topic: _____

_____

Introductory statement: _____

_____

Fact 1: _____

_____

_____

Fact 2: _____

_____

_____

Fact 3: _____

_____

_____

Question: _____

_____

Conclusion: _____

_____

Name _____

Draw your own manga character in the centre of the web.
Write sentences in the boxes around the picture to describe its features.

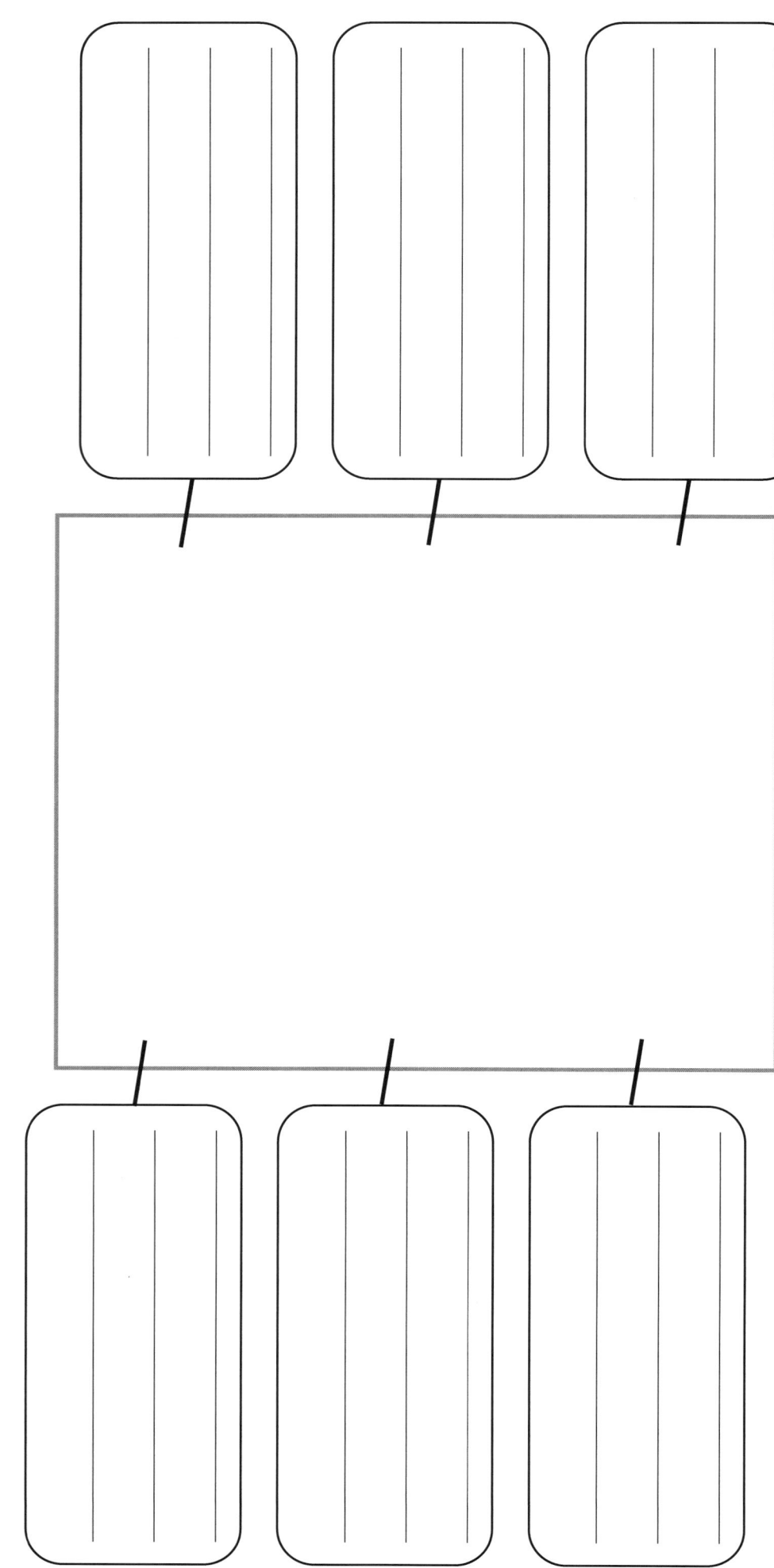

PCM
15

How to Make Manga Characters
Learning objective: Integrate words and images imaginatively for different purposes.

© HarperCollins*Publishers* 2009.
This page may be photocopied for use in the classroom.

Name _____

Chose a design in the book that you liked.
Create a fact file for it, and include
a picture of it.

Design fact file

Name of building: _____

_____

Who designed it: _____

_____

Where it's located: _____

_____

Special design features:

- _____

- _____

- _____

- _____

Collins Big Cat and guided reading

What is guided reading?

A guided reading lesson usually takes place with a teacher and a small group of children at roughly the same attainment level. It is a vital part of the teaching of reading, being the step between shared reading with explicit reading instruction and independent reading.

The lesson revolves around one book, which with Sapphire and Diamond titles may be read over more than one session. Each child in the group has their own copy. The teacher may introduce children to the book in a variety of ways. The children could start by browsing through the book and discussing their ideas of what it's about. Alternatively, the teacher could explicitly model reading strategies for comprehension. In this way, children learn to become independent readers. Speaking and listening is still a vital part of the reading process at this level. It helps children to make explicit their own knowledge and understanding of texts and also know themselves as readers.

Selecting the right book for the group's reading level and interest level is vital. In the context of guided reading, the children should be able to read about 90% of the text easily. The remaining 10% of the book presents a challenge to the children and offers a focused teaching and learning opportunity which forms the basis of the lesson. *Collins Big Cat* supports selection

of the correct book by banding each book to indicate the reading level. The book can also reflect the children's learning needs assessed prior to choosing the book. In this way the children should read fluently, with engagement, while developing specific reading strategies. At this level these include inference and deduction, as well as the ability to critically evaluate, summarise and question. Children have the opportunity to further develop their reading stamina and critical skills across a range of text types.

A guided reading session generally comprises four parts:

1. **Getting started**: The *introduction to the new book*, led by the teacher, which paves the way for the children's independent reading of the book. This is a good time to remind children of strategies that they can use.

2. **Reading and responding**: *The independent reading of all or part of the book by each child.* This is facilitated by the teacher who supports children reading with increasing fluency, stamina and independence, as they tackle what may be unfamiliar concepts and new vocabulary. The teacher may set follow-on activities that develop skills such as questioning, inference and deduction, which are increasingly important to developing readers. These activities may be returned to at the next guided reading session.

3. **Returning to the text**: A *rereading of parts of the book*, led by the teacher, who will help children to demonstrate their understanding of the book using a variety of strategies such as group discussion, drama techniques or giving a presentation. This may involve reflecting on themselves as readers and describing their progress. In this way, the teacher is able to assess what the children have learnt and help to consolidate learning.

4. **Checking and moving on**: A *follow-up activity* that consolidates the learning objective of the guided reading session. This can be a group, paired or individual activity, for instance further research to support work in other curriculum areas.

Of course, every book is different, but here are some guidelines to approaching a guided reading session. These guidelines have been adopted by *Collins Big Cat*, and every title has a suggested guided reading plan at the back (*Ideas for guided reading*).

1. Getting started

The book introduction is a key part of the guided reading session. It works best if you know the book reasonably well, and are aware of where challenges may arise, as well as the learning objectives to focus on.

Developing readers will draw from many different life experiences, for example some children will know about the Solar System and will bring this prior knowledge to help them understand the book *The Traveller's Guide to the Solar System* (Sapphire/ Band 16). You will need to orientate children with varying degrees of knowledge of the world to the book. Discussion is a good way to do this, for example, children can share what they know about the Solar System in order to predict possible content and raise questions that will support engagement. Images from the book and artefacts can play an important part in building a bridge between children's prior knowledge and what is

new. For example, children can learn a lot from scanning photographs and illustrations in *Hard Times* (Diamond/Band 17), which describes what life was like for children living in Victorian times.

Independent and guided browsing, including reading the cover and title pages, will activate children's prior knowledge, familiarise the children with text and structure and heighten their awareness of unfamiliar vocabulary. The purpose of this part of the session is to reduce uncertainty and prepare children to actively engage with the book as they complete reading tasks.

During the book introduction, you can model a variety of skills and attitudes to reading. For example, when reading a non-fiction book, you might comment on the quality of the photography, or model how to deal with new concepts such as changes to the environment, by showing children how to raise questions about the subject and deal with unfamiliar words. In reading fiction, the book may require children to make inferences and engage with increasingly literary and figurative language. You can model how to read aloud for comic and dramatic effect and develop children's abilities to offer their own perspective on the author's intentions.

2. Reading and responding

In guided reading at this level, you will set learning objectives and tasks. Children may spend time reading away from you, developing autonomy before returning to discuss their ideas.

For example, they may be required to read a certain number of chapters in order to discuss some of their ideas about the author's intentions. Several chapters may need to be read before the children can make a character sketch or understand attitudes. You can model how to tackle the tasks that you are setting, for example to analyse Philip's and his family's feelings about moving from London after World War II with reference to the book *Moving Out* (Diamond/Band 17). Children are required to read independently or in pairs to engage with the task in hand. Speaking and listening and recording ideas using notes may be an integral part of reading and responding. Children should be encouraged to share effective strategies for making meaning and identify any problems that they encounter. You can monitor progress and support children as necessary. You may choose to hear individual readers in order to assess progress, or encourage children to evaluate themselves as readers.

3. Returning to the book

When the children have finished reading independently, there is an opportunity to talk about the book together. Learning objectives can be consolidated, for example, children may discuss what they have learnt about a character as a result of their reading. This is an ideal opportunity for the group to share and justify their ideas and develop their ability to infer and deduce in relation to the book shared, other related texts and their own life experiences. In both fiction and non-fiction, evaluating a book is an important part

of establishing a critical attitude to reading. For non-fiction books, children may evaluate the book with reference to its purpose, for example does *Fragile Earth* (Diamond/Band 17) persuade us that the world's climate is really changing? For fiction, children may be encouraged to respond critically to issues raised in stories, finding evidence in the book and exploring alternative courses of action. Evaluating the author's solution to the character's dilemma is a way of thinking about an author's intentions. In *The Monkey Puppet* (Sapphire/Band 16) a tension chart helps readers explore how the author structures the story. Drama techniques such as hot-seating and freeze frame can be useful ways of deepening response and engaging children as speakers and listeners. The reading response pages are designed specifically to help children summarise information and reflect upon the book.

4. Checking and moving on

At the end of the guided reading session the main focus should be on reinforcing the learning objectives. It is also an opportunity to link the guided reading session to work done in other areas of the curriculum. The conclusion of the guided reading session may be delayed as children read and work on the books in their own time or in other lessons. If guided reading involves several sessions working on one book, the conclusion will draw on work from all those sessions. The purpose of the checking and moving on section is to engage children in activities that help consolidate and extend new learning. Activities could include links with other areas of the curriculum, for example, Citizenship, Art, History, Science and Design Technology. Speaking and listening activities can help children present what they have learnt to different audiences. *Ideas for guided reading* at the back of every *Collins Big Cat* book provide a range of ideas for follow-up activities. This Assessment and Support guide also provides photocopy masters for further activities (see pp34–49).

Collins Big Cat book bands and progression

The key to successful guided reading sessions is skilful selection of the appropriate book for a particular child or group of children. Each book should provide neither too little nor too much challenge for the reader.

The goal of guided reading is for children to read accurately, with enjoyment, putting into practice appropriate reading strategies while thinking about the meaning of the book. Within the context of guided reading, if the book presents too much of a challenge (e.g. where the child makes more than one error in every ten words) then the child's reading may lose fluency, phrasing and motivation. If the book presents too little challenge then the child is not reading at an appropriate level for making progress.

Collins Big Cat supports teachers by grading each book clearly. Collins Big Cat books are graded into 18 bands of progressive difficulty, from the simplest wordless books at Lilac/0 level to books for fluent readers at Diamond/17. These bands are similar to the level-by-level rationale of Book Bands for Guided Reading (Bickler, Baker and Hobsbaum). Collins Big Cat banding helps the teacher match suitable reading books to a child's reading ability level, invaluable in planning guided reading sessions. There is a book banding summary from Copper/12 to Diamond/17 on the inside back cover of this guide.

Managing progression in guided reading

Guided reading works most effectively when the children in a group are working at a similar level on an appropriate book which offers the right amount of challenge. Careful assessment enables the teacher to put the children into ability groups and to identify the appropriate level of Collins Big Cat for each group.

An effective way of assessing which band is appropriate for a child is by filling in a **Reading Skills Sheet** (see pp60 to 63) as the child reads a book at a level which you consider most suits their reading experience. These sheets outline the reading skills a child should be able to

Collins Big Cat book bands at Year 5/6/Scottish P4/5 stage
Working towards National Curriculum Level 4 (Sapphire)
Working within National Curriculum Level 4 (Diamond)
Scottish Curriculum for Excellence Second Stage (reading, talking, writing, listening)

Book band	Learning opportunities	Text features	Approximate word count
Sapphire Band 16	Decodes new and unfamiliar words and deduces meaning from the context. Understands and internalises text organisation of a widening range of genres. Recognises how authors create different effects. Develops a questioning, active response to texts that is based on personal response and empathy. Understands how response can change with reading over time.	Quite complex sentence structures with wider vocabulary and conventional line breaks in both fiction and non-fiction.	4000
Diamond Band 17	Integrates and applies a wide range of independent skills and adapts skills consciously to suit different reading purposes. Develops an active and critical response to texts with a growing awareness of multiple possible themes and meanings. Understands how perceptions change over time with reading. Recognises how authors use sophisticated devices to influence readers.	More complex sentence structures with ever widening vocabulary in both fiction and non-fiction.	5000

demonstrate at each book band. High scores in most of these categories suggest the child be placec at a higher band, average or low scores that the child should continue in this band or even move to an easier band.

Checking progression

Children make progress at different rates and often in spurts. Useful indicators of how suited children are to a reading level are:

- fluency in reading
- comprehension of the book
- ability to explore underlying themes and ideas making reference to text and authorial intentions
- stamina in reading extended texts and chapter books
- ability to respond to and evaluate books read.

A child's progress in these skills can be checked in the **Reading Skills Sheets** (see pp60 to 63)

at regular intervals. These sheets provide a basis for you to observe and assess which skills the child has mastered and which still need to be developed or consolidated, and decide whether the child should move bands. They also give you the opportunity to identify and intervene where a particular weakness is holding back a child's progress.

It is a good idea to periodically recheck each child's reading skills, using these or your own school's assessment sheets, every six weeks or so, and regroup or reband children if necessary. A child who consistently reads fluently and with comprehension, which enables them to infer and deduce beyond the literal, might be moved up a level. Decoding skills should be firmly established at this level. However, miscues may occur as children encounter new and challenging vocabulary. If a child makes regular miscues with high frequency and familiar words, this may be a sign that the text is too challenging. In this case,

Sapphire/Band 16

Sapphire/Band 16

the child may need to revisit the previous band. Similarly a child who is losing the sense of what they read may be moved down a level. Children will vary in the amount of time that they spend with a particular level.

Assessment can be supported by using the **Individual ongoing records** on pp58–59 or the **Ongoing Group Record Sheet** on p64.

Collins Big Cat bands

At *Collins Big Cat* Sapphire/Band 16 the fiction books include both longer chapter books and anthologies of short stories to develop children's sustained engagement with texts. Increased syntactic complexity allows readers to experience advanced literary conventions and understand how language is used for effect, with reference to other times and places enabling them to explore a range of cultural issues and different writers' perspectives. The non-fiction texts complement these themes with a range of information texts and non-chronological reports, which examine not just our own past and present world but, in *The Traveller's Guide to the Solar System*, the world beyond Earth. The use of more complex maps and diagrams requires readers to develop their retrieval and research skills.

At *Collins Big Cat* Diamond/Band 17 the extended chapter books and collections of short stories offer more thematic, as well as literary, complexity to provide opportunities for readers to understand causes and points of view. As well as exploring experiences from different times and places, the sophistication of language styles enables readers to engage with, and begin to question, the author's intentions. The non-fiction texts support this social, moral and cultural exploration through a selection of books which enable readers to gain understanding about where and how people live.

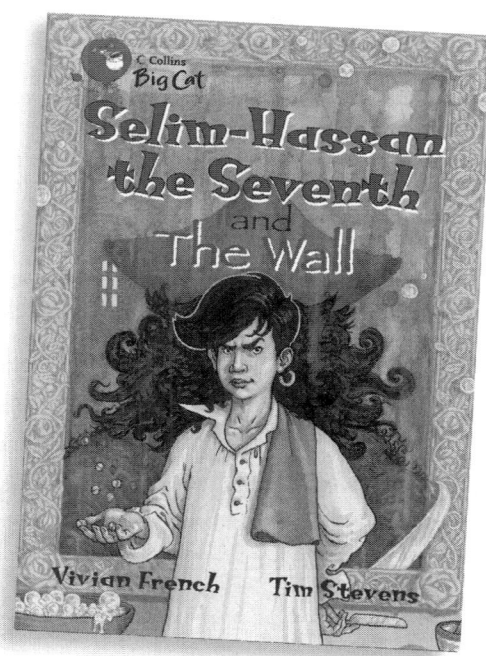

Diamond/Band 17

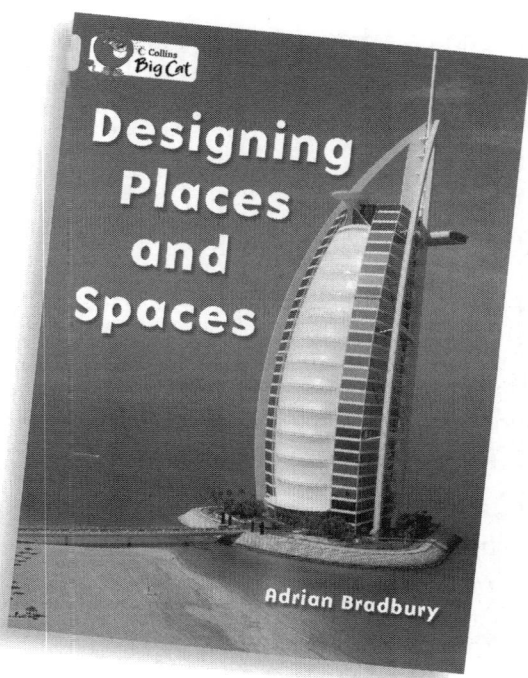

Diamond/Band 17

Ideas for assessment

The key to good assessment is to identify each child's strengths and weaknesses followed by immediate intervention and/or further teaching. The photocopiable assessment and planning sheets provided in the *Collins Big Cat Assessment and Support Guide* are designed to help with this.

What is reading assessment?

At this level, assessment of reading will include observing children's confidence and attitudes to reading, as well as noting the strategies that they use or do not use to make meaning. In addition to listening to children read, discussion before and after reading will help you to establish whether children are using skills of inference and deduction and developing critical evaluation skills, as well as decoding at a literal level. Assessment of reading progress can take many forms and relies upon evidence from a range of sources gathered within and beyond the guided reading session. Your observations during the guided reading session can be recorded using the skills sheets on pp60–63 and these may complement children's informal written and dramatic/oral responses to texts. These skills sheets can be used as a record of achievement and may also provide evidence for structured periodic assessment systems such as AP³ (Assessing Pupil Progress), where pupils' ongoing work and progress towards National Curriculum levels for reading can be reviewed. All of this information can be used to inform future teaching and planning.

Preparing for the reading session

Before working with a book in a guided reading session, it is important to identify which learning opportunities are offered by it, and what you will be looking for in the children's reading and response to the book. *Collins Big Cat* books have learning objectives and ideas for guided reading provided at the back of every book in the *Ideas for guided reading* section.

When using the books with a guided reading group, you can refer to this to help you assess, for example, children's ability to develop a questioning, active response to text that is based on personal response and empathy.

During the reading session

Although assessment should be continuous, only significant strengths and weaknesses need to be noted for each child, related to what is being taught. Many weaknesses can be corrected immediately by good intervention from teachers. For example, open questions and involving dialogue help children to think about their learning and their next steps for improvement. Although you may not listen to each child read aloud at this age, some children, when reaching difficult parts of text, may read quietly under their breath. This can be an effective strategy to support decoding.

After the reading session

Used systematically and analytically, *Collins Big Cat* assessment stimulates reading progress by focusing planning on the significant weakness of individual children and/or groups. Identified weakness can be rectified between guided reading sessions by one-to-one intervention from teachers, teaching assistants, or by homework and parental help. Intervention is essential to the assessment process. It increases children's reading confidence, and accelerates learning in the time available for guided reading.

Remember that children may progress at different rates. Continuous assessment helps you to identify when attainment groups need to be re-formed, as will happen from time to time. For example, some children will read silently with sustained concentration and return to it easily after a break, while other children need support to do this.

Progression

As children progress between reading levels, observe how they cope with the increasing level of complexity in terms of both book and learning objectives. Additionally, you may need to evaluate and note the characteristics of individual children. Perhaps some children ask sensible questions about the book, while others rely too heavily on one reading strategy. Children are making good progress when showing sustained interest in the book when reading silently and completing a related activity that develops understanding.

Above all, children must show good understanding of the books they are reading, whether fiction or non-fiction, demonstrating this, for example, through their questions, discussion and response. The reading response pages at the end of each *Collins Big Cat* book give you an immediate "way in" to checking overall understanding, and to discussion.

Collins Big Cat assessment support

The reading response pages in every *Collins Big Cat* guided reading book offer an immediate assessment opportunity for teachers. They are designed to stimulate children's discussion and recapping of a text which allows you to check and assess children's comprehension of what they have just read.

During each guided reading session, a teacher using the photocopiable **Individual ongoing records** (pp58–59) can note each child's particular weaknesses and strengths, and then identify the necessary action needed to rectify weaknesses and to build on strengths. For example, an improving and confident reader might be offered a supported extension activity, such as Internet research. A hesitant reader might require direct teaching of a reading skill, perhaps additional strategies for solving unfamiliar words or using an information retrieval device effectively. Children in either category might benefit from a move to a reading band more closely matched to their attainment level.

The **Individual ongoing records** are linked to each *Collins Big Cat* book band, and provide generic band objectives. You can check that children reading at any level are meeting band objectives while fulfilling the learning objectives specific to each book.

The **Reading Skills Sheets** (pp60–63) provide a method of matching a child's attainment to a suitable book band, and can also be used to check that children are reading at the correct level. The sheets should not be used for ongoing assessment, but as a periodic check that a child has progressed in various key reading skills. The sheets can be used similarly to reading records, noting intervention or teaching action related to a child's difficulties in acquiring a specific reading skill. Each reading skill has been cross referenced with National Curriculum Assessment Focuses (AFs) for reading to support structured periodic assessment.

Collins Big Cat's **Resources and Records Manager CD-ROM** provides a convenient, efficient and paper-free way to keep records for each child's or group's progress and reading history. These can be used to inform the choice of intervention and help with selecting appropriate books to support individual children or groups.

In addition, the **Ongoing Group Record Sheet** (p64) and **Half-Termly Group Assessment Sheet** (p66) allow the teacher to summarise a child's progress over a longer period as well as monitor the progress of each group as a whole. (Written samples showing how these sheets can be used are also provided on pages 65 and 67 respectively.) These can be used in conjunction with **Half-Termly Planning Notes** (p68. Sample on p69).

Individual ongoing record (Sapphire/Band 16)

Collins **Big Cat**

Name _____   **Group** _____

At Sapphire look to see if the reader:

- decodes new and unfamiliar words and deduces meaning from the context
- understands and internalises text organisation of a widening range of genres
- recognises how authors create different effects
- develops a questioning, active response to texts that is based on personal response and empathy
- understands how response can change with reading over time.

Date/book	Session objectives	Specific strengths and weaknesses	Next steps

Individual ongoing record (Diamond/Band 17)

Name _____ **Group** _____

At Diamond look to see if the reader:
- integrates and applies a wide range of independent skills and adapts skills consciously to suit different reading purposes
- develops an active and critical response to texts, with a growing awareness of multiple possible themes and meanings
- understands how perceptions change over time with reading
- recognises how authors use sophisticated devices to influence readers.

Date/book	Session objectives	Specific strengths and weaknesses	Next steps

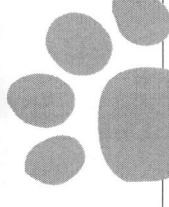

Collins Big Cat Assessment and Support Guide F

Individual Fiction Reading Skills Sheet (Sapphire/Band 16)

Name _____ **Group** _____

Skill (Assessment Focus)	Score*	Action
Uses knowledge of words, roots, derivations and spelling patterns to read unknown words **AF1**		
Understands how stories may vary, e.g. in pace, build-up, sequence, complication and resolution **AF4,7**		
Uses knowledge of stories to make and confirm predictions of structure and content while reading **AF3,4**		
Identifies features of different fiction genres, e.g. science fiction, adventure, myths, legends **AF7**		
Identifies the point of view from which a story is told and responds, e.g. by retelling from a different point of view **AF3,6**		
Understands the difference between literal and figurative language, and how it is used to achieve an effect **AF5**		
Recognises how characters are presented in different ways and responds to this with reference to the text **AF2,3**		
Infers meaning with reference to the text and also applying wider experience **AF3,7**		
Develops an active and questioning response to reading, e.g. by empathising with characters, imagining events **AF3**		
Takes part in peer-group discussions and is prepared to widen reading experience based on recommendation **AF7**		

*Score key
1 = struggling
2 = progressing
3 = skill secured

Collins Big Cat Assessment and Support Guide F

Individual Non-fiction Reading Skills Sheet (Sapphire/Band 16)

Name _____   Group _____

Skill (Assessment Focus)	Score*	Action
Uses knowledge of words, roots, derivations and spelling patterns to read unknown words **AF1**		
Uses knowledge of non-fiction texts to make and confirm predictions of structure and content while reading **AF4**		
Knows structures and grammatical features of a range of non-fiction text-types, e.g. non-chronological reports, persuasive texts **AF4,7**		
Makes use of features that enable the reader to locate specific information, e.g. contents, sections, headings **AF2,4**		
Locates information confidently and efficiently using appropriate skills, e.g. skimming and scanning **AF2**		
Evaluates texts critically by comparing and evaluating how the information is presented **AF4,7**		
Develops an active response by raising questions and connecting reading to wider experiences **AF3,7**		
Uses the blurb and cover information to appraise the contents quickly **AF2**		
Takes part in peer discussions and is prepared to widen reading experience based on discussion **AF7**		

*Score key
1 = struggling
2 = progressing
3 = skill secured

Individual Fiction Reading Skills Sheet (Diamond/Band 17)

Name _____   Group _____

Skill (Assessment Focus)	Score*	Action
Uses knowledge of word derivations and word formation to construct the meaning of more challenging words in context **AF1**		
Reads fluently, understanding and using more sophisticated punctuation marks, e.g. colon, semicolon **AF5**		
Understands the use of connectives as signposts to indicate a change of tone or voice and applies this to maintain understanding **AF5**		
Identifies and describes the styles of authors **AF4,6**		
Distinguishes between implicit and explicit points of view **AF3**		
Comments on the success of texts and writers in evoking particular responses from the reader **AF6**		
Analyses how moods, feelings and attitudes are conveyed, using inference and deduction **AF3**		
Makes reference to the text and wider understanding when discussing opinions **AF7**		
Comments critically on the overall impact of the text with reference to a range of features, e.g. use of language, range of themes **AF4,5,6**		
Declares and justifies personal preferences for authors and types of text **AF7**		

*Score key
1 = struggling
2 = progressing
3 = skill secured

Collins Big Cat Assessment and Support Guide F

Individual Non-fiction Reading Skills Sheet (Diamond/Band 17)

Name _____ **Group** _____

Skill (Assessment Focus)	Score*	Action
Uses knowledge of word derivations and word formation to construct the meaning of more challenging words in context **AF1**		
Applies grammatical knowledge when rereading more complex sentences **AF5**		
Understands the use of connectives as signposts to indicate a change of opinion and applies this to maintain understanding when reading information texts **AF5**		
Uses secure understanding of the language features and structures of the full range of non-fiction text types to support understanding when reading **AF4**		
Secures the skills of skimming and scanning and efficient reading so that research is fast and effective **AF2**		
Appraises and evaluates a text quickly and effectively **AF2,3**		
Considers the viewpoint of the author and possible alternative versions **AF6,7**		
Decides on the quality/usefulness of a text by skim-reading to gain an overall impression **AF2,6**		
Declares and justifies personal preferences for authors and types of non-fiction text **AF7**		

*Score key
1 = struggling
2 = progressing
3 = skill secured

Ongoing Group Record Sheet

Group _____   Term _____

Names:

Skills already attained by children:

Learning targets:

Week	Book (band)	Focus	Progress towards learning target
1			
2			
3			
4			
5			
6			

*Score key
1 = struggling
2 = progressing
3 = skill secured

Collins Big Cat Assessment and Support Guide F

Ongoing Group Record Sheet (sample)

Group **Red**   Term **Easter 2008**

Names:

Niah, Owen, Maisy, Jacob

Skills already attained by children:

- Uses knowledge of stories to make + confirm predictions.
- Makes use of features to locate specific information.
- Identifies + describes the styles of authors.

Learning targets:

A. Identifies features of different fiction genres.
B. Uses the blurb + cover information to appraise the contents quickly.
C. Distinguishes between implicit + explicit points of view.
D. Appraises + evaluates a text quickly + effectively.

Week	Book (band)	Focus	Progress towards learning target
1	The Golden Turtle and Other Tales (Sapphire)	Identifies features of different fiction genres; Distinguishes between implicit + explicit points of view.	All identified features of the genre ③ Niah + Jacob were able to distinguish between implicit + explicit points of view ③ Owen + Maisy needed help identifying implicit points of view ②
2	The Monkey Puppet (Sapphire)	Identifies features of different fiction genres; Uses the blurb + cover to appraise contents quickly.	Good group discussion on the genre ③ Niah, Owen + Jacob struggled to appraise the contents using the blurb + cover ① Maisy successfully appraised the contents ③
3	The Ultimate World Quiz (Sapphire)	Uses the blurb + cover information to appraise contents quickly; Appraises + evaluates a text quickly + effectively.	All used the blurb + cover to appraise the contents ③ Maisy + Jacob evaluated the text quickly ③ while Niah + Owen struggled ①
4	Selim - Hassan The Seventh + The Wall (Diamond)	Identifies features of different fiction genres; Distinguishes between implicit + explicit points of view.	Despite good group discussion, all struggled to identify features of genre ① Niah + Jacob distinguished between implicit + explicit views ③ Maisy + Owen struggled to identify either ①
5	Hard Times (Diamond)	Uses the blurb + cover information to appraise the contents quickly; Appraises + evaluates a text quickly + effectively.	All used the cover + blurb to appraise the contents successfully ③ Maisy + Jacob struggled to evaluate the contents ① Niah + Owen did well ②
6	Fragile Earth (Diamond)	Distinguishes between implicit + explicit points of view; Appraises + evaluates a text quickly + effectively	Niah + Jacob did well distinguishing between implicit + explicit points of view ③ Maisy + Owen made good progress with this ② good group discussion on the text ③

© HarperCollins*Publishers* 2009. This page may be photocopied for use in the classroom.

*Score key
1 = struggling
2 = progressing
3 = skill secured

Half-termly Group Assessment Sheet

Class _____ Term _____ Group _____ Book band _____

Group objectives _____

Child's name	Books used and date	Reading	Responding to text	Evaluation and next steps

Next objectives _____

Review date _____

Collins Big Cat Assessment and Support Guide F

Half-termly Group Assessment Sheet (sample)

Class _6J_

Term _Summer 2008_   Group _Red_   Book band _Diamond_

Group objectives _Declares + justifies personal preferences for authors + types of text; Applies grammatical knowledge when reading more complex sentences_

Child's name	Books used and date	Reading	Responding to text	Evaluation and next steps
Jaidah	Moving Out 5/6, 12/6	Reads fluently uses a range of strategies unprompted.	Good comprehension skills forthcoming in group discussing + can support personal opinions very well.	Attained all objectives).
George	Fearless Flynn and Other Tales 19/6, 26/6	Reads fluently uses a range of strategies.	Enjoyed reading short stories, struggled to justify his preferences.	Read more fiction and try to identify personal preferences.
Megan	Fragile Earth 3/7, 10/7	Reads fairly fluently. Struggles with unfamiliar words.	Enjoyed reading non-fiction but becomes demotivated when struggling with tricky words.	Needs more practice at this level - read more big/small fiction books together.
Greg	How to Make Manga Characters 17/7, 24/7	Reads fluently self-correctly when he makes a mistake.	Enjoyed reading fiction + non-fiction. Showing good understanding but very quiet in group discussions.	Offer support + encouragement during group discussions to build his confidence.

Review date _1st Aug 2008_   Next objectives _Makes reference to the text + wider understanding when discussing opinions; Considers the viewpoint of the author + possible alternative versions_

Half-termly Planning Notes

Collins **Big Cat**

Class _____   Term _____   Group _____

Session sequence	Session 1	Session 2	Session 3	Session 4	Session 5	Session 6
Book title						
Getting started						
Reading and responding						
Returning to the book						
Checking and moving on						

Half-termly Planning Notes (sample)

Class **6J**   Term **3**   Group **Red**

Session sequence	Session 1	Session 2	Session 3	Session 4	Session 5	Session 6
Book title	Moving Out	Moving Out	Fearless Flynn	Fearless Flynn	Fragile Earth	Fragile Earth
Getting started	Look at the cover + blurb together + discuss what the book might be about. Describe the Blitz + post-war London.	Recap the story so far + discuss Philip's point of view.	Share some spooky tales with each other + discuss some of the features of spooky stories.	Recount the story + revisit the speeches that make it spooky.	Look at the cover + blurb together + discuss what the book might be about + what the author's purpose might be.	Recap some of the issues raised in the book so far.
Reading and responding	Children to read chapters 1+2, thinking about how Philip's point of view changes. Children go into role as Philip.	Group continues reading to the end of the story silently.	Read the opening of Fearless Flynn + discuss the ways the author has used for effect. Children predict what might happen.	Children to read the opening of the story silently. Discuss what features the author has used to make it spooky.	Read the opening pages. Children to select a topic from the contents page, read it + write preparation for a presentation.	Children to read to the end of the book silently.
Returning to the book	Children share ideas about why Philip's point of view changed + discuss other characters' views.	Recount the story + discuss the different points of view. Children go into role as different characters.	Children to read to the end of the story silently. Discuss the ways the language + hence impact + suspense are created.	Children discuss how the stories are different + similar, exploring how suspense + impact are created in each one.	Ask children to share the information they found + discuss different ways to find information in a book.	Discuss a question about one of the topics shared + ask children to investigate it further.
Checking and moving on	(next session)	Children create an advert for a New Town.	(next session)	Children record a reading of Fearless Flynn as a play for the radio.	(next session)	Children prepare for a presentation on the "Fragile Earth".

© HarperCollinsPublishers 2009.
This page may be photocopied for use in the classroom.

Fiction Book Review Sheet

Book title _____

Author _____

What I thought about this book

Setting

Characters

What happens

Non-fiction Book Review Sheet

Book title _____

Author _____

What this book is about

What I knew (K)

What I learned (L)

What I want to find out now (F)

This book includes:

contents	☐	diagrams	☐	photographs	☐
captions	☐	tables	☐	fact boxes	☐
glossary	☐	index	☐		

Notes